LIGN SERIES / 4

Kerala Journal

Kim Dorman

XYLEM BOOKS 2021

LIGN SERIES

LS1   Oliver Southall, *Borage Blue*
LS2   Gerry Loose, *The Great Book of the Woods*
LS3   Jennifer Spector, *Hithe*
LS4   Kim Dorman, *Kerala Journal*

Kim Dorman, *Kerala Journal*
First published in 2021 by Xylem Books

All content © Kim Dorman 2021
The author's moral rights have been asserted
This edition © Xylem Books 2021

Cover image by Kim Dorman

ISBN: 978-1-9163935-5-4

Xylem Books is an imprint of Corbel Stone Press

I

12

II

27

III

49

IV

121

Author's Notes

169

Kerala Journal

The sun is broad (like a leaf).
Anaximenes

I

Nightfall. Rats scamper
in the attic. The sinuous notes
of a nadaswaram drift
from the nearby temple.
On the road, buses carry pilgrims
to Sabarimala. The winter air
is crisp. Numberless insects
chant to the stars.

atop a tall
wooden post
at the edge

of the paddy field,
a small blue
kingfisher

looks down,
watching
the water

My next door
neighbour tills his
small plot;
from the east
the smell of rain.

a light
blue shard
lies among
pebbles

overhead,
racket-tailed
drongos
spin, chase

The cool season has come;
work begins
on houses, roads.

Piles of dead
leaves slowly burn.

As the long day fades, we
turn to the west.

Fruit bats fly toward the sun.

glimpse of
a small green
parakeet

for a moment
in the silk
cotton tree

Clouds in the east
like gilded rags.

Before sunrise,
silent birds cross the sky.

This morning
we sat on the stone steps
in a cool breeze.

In the garden white
flowers (a kind of lily?)
attracted swarms

of tiny black bees.

down from
the sky

each crow

finds
a branch

Rain drips on the
tin roof, frogs
& crickets chant.

The passing days
turn to years.

Lying awake in the
dark, I know the
taste of ash.

Evening is still as rain clouds
rise in the west. All the trees
are dark silhouettes: teak, jack,
coconut. The world is silent
but for the echoing cry
of a brainfever bird.

Far thunder recedes. Gray
light reflects from paddy fields.

What is the name of that flower,
dark as blood, dripping rain?

The clogged gutters overflow.
A silent crow flies past.

The rain has stopped,
darkness comes:
the day ends. Lamps
are lit in certain homes;
the fine scent of
hot coconut oil fills
the still air. At the end
of every wick, a white
immaterial pearl.
Luminous, steady ...

—for Ella

II

Sandhya. Crickets
begin their vespers.
On the doorstep an oil
lamp glows. Rats
gnaw at wood beams
in the attic, dust settles
on table & chairs.
A pale, transparent gecko
clings to the wall.

Venus appears over
the cowshed

like an ancient sign.

I walk back from the
post office in sweltering
heat. Two men squat
by a trestle cart
and spit. A shiny black
crow whets its beak
on a rock. At the curve,
speeding lorries raise dust.

in the cool
night

air,
flowers

curl up,
as if

sleeping

Dusk: the hiss of a gas
lamp. Across the canal,
bunches of red, yellow
& green bananas
hang in a fruit stall.

That bird,
master of notes
& pauses.

At the tap
a hollow bucket
fills.

Midday heat.
The pebble sound of chickpeas
poured into a pot.

Midnight. The shops
and stalls near the train
station are open.
Pilgrims crowd the streets.
Buses, scooters, bicycles,
auto-rickshaws. Smell of urine,
fried food, incense. Dogs
wander unnoticed.

The day fades.
A humid breeze carries
the stench of paddy fields.
Living in the moment,
a crow cocks its head
& looks at me.

the sound
of unseen
rain

Daybreak. Pilgrims
throng the train station.
Black-clad men lie
next to sacred bundles.
Many are asleep.
Others squat in circles
sharing food. They
are barefoot & unshaved.
The sun appears above
the trees. Descending
onto littered tracks, crows
scavenge, fight. Smoke
hangs over the platform.

Clear sound of a conch
from the temple. Day's colours
fade in the paddy field's
dark mirror. A pond
heron rises from the ditch.

in darkness
the light
of bones

I drip sweat
loading
roof tiles

into the back
of an auto-
rickshaw,

quietly
observed
by an

old man &
a dog.

I toss a small
stone

into the river.

A kingfisher
sees it

too,

in silence.

Power lines trail in the dust.
A dead flying fox lies on the path.
Boys ride by on bicycles.

The daylight fades.
A distant nadaswaram.

Waking & dream balance a void,
wrote Thompson.

Each shadow, an abyss.

blind dog
lies
apart

III

Drifting to sleep in the afternoon. Birdsong
like constellations. Sunlight on water.

Gold light
on the wing tips & breast feathers
of a hawk-eagle

flying low toward the river.

Twilight on the
vanishing
path: the rock
wall split
apart
by a tree's
snake-
like
roots.

My neighbour and his
two young sons
hoe a path
in front of their house.

A dead flying fox hangs
tangled in electric
cables over the roof.

Nature's rhythms
are slow.
Yet in a blink
the quick is still.

we stare into the wound

Reek of garbage &
the urine stench from
concrete walls. A pariah
dog slinks past. I limp home
with a broken sandal.
Gate half-hidden by lush
bougainvillea.

waning yellow
gibbous

cat's eye
moon

The night is humid, still.
If I stand by the open window
I can see the moon.
A lorry rumbles by on the road.
The years pass quickly.
Already another is gone.

the moon
a yellow
crescent

could be
a bowl
or a boat

Morning's heat. I fill a bucket
to water the garden, listen
to birdsong & the migrant
wind. Sunlight pours through a leaf,
fire, water on dust. The
names in your head. Nilgiri
pipit. Nilgiri thrush.

Roadside fruit stand:
bananas, mangoes,
coconuts, limes.
Machine to crush
sugarcane. A boy
offers glasses of juice.

This morning's
light rain.

Dust laid,
the path's scent.

Blurred moon rises in the west.
Darkness all around and a few lights
beyond the paddy field. I light incense.
My lamp is dim as if clouds and smoke
filled the room, bringing voices
of people I don't know and far off
a dog barking.

bending
in

a breeze
then

rising,
as

if
lifted

In evening twilight
the silent passage
of great winged bats.

A narrow path
skirts the temple.

Wild jackfruits lie
rotting amid
footprints in dust.

By the gate, a tall
copper flagstaff
glistens

in the midday sun.

birds
swim
in air

In the moonless dark
night sounds
fill a hollow space.

Empty, the dog's bark,
hum of the road,
a cicada's thin whine.

Open the shutters
of the heart.

Smoky silver light.
The weight of a green papaya.

The temple gates
are shut.

Wayside shops
are closed.

No scooters, cars,
or trucks.

A man leans
on a parapet wall.

Ash-coloured clouds
float by.

My window
looks out
on the sky.

I see what
it sees.

The rain has stopped.
I wrap myself

in a cotton shawl
& step out into the cool air

on the veranda.
A million frogs sing as one

in the flooded paddies.
Venus shines clear.

Dark path, dim torch—
I'm startled by the call
of a frogmouth.

The chemist
hands me a bottle
wrapped in
newsprint—
the obituaries.

The rhythm of chendas
echoes downstream.
Gods and heroes dance
in the night. We walk home
under rain-wet trees. The
waxing gibbous moon is
obscured by a cloud.

A one-horn
rhino
ambled

28 km,
met no people
en route.

The Hindu
March 29, 2020

I walk home
each night
at the same hour.

Venus
shines in the west.

Some nights silver
others
pale gold.

By the paddy bund
an old man
grows melons.

Hair white, thin,
I bend painfully
in the garden.
All around,
neighbours gossip.
Crows flock to the trees.

That single rose
in the twilight garden
has the radiance
of a dream.

the crushed leaf
the cut root
the shattered stone

the sound
is a rain of
blossoms

Things begin to shut down.
Not the spiders at work in the rafters.

Among my books
are three versions of Herakleitos.

silvery crow
hunched
in the rain

On the dusty path a small snake is threatened by a crow

.

Walking home with a musk melon

.

Lockdown, my sudden wish for an old children's book

.

In cool wind, I tend a leaf fire as it rains

.

Braiding their flight two butterflies over the garden

.

On the path unseen silken threads touch my face

.

Storm's boon: a coconut by the gate

in the
silence
after
dark

rain
drips
from
the trees

There's
no electricity.

My neighbours
read to their child
by candlelight.

Like we used to do.

—for my son

Sitting on a grass mat, I look up from a book
to discuss important matters. Roof tiles dislodged
by a palm civet. The water level in the well.
A missing shirt button.

mornings
make visible
dusty
cobwebs

A bird's single
high-
pitched note,
repeated.

A crow drinks
from the rain gutter,
jumps in the air
and is gone.

A farmer clears his field with a sickle.
Fodder for cows.

On the road, a young family goes past
on a scooter.

Man, woman, child.

we lived here once
climbed these steps

stood on this stoop
looked at these walls

slept here, ate here
laughed cried

the tang of memory

moon adrift
the humid night
a dream of night

Fruit and vegetable stalls
line Market Road.
Squatting beside his cart,
the vendor wears a bandana
over his nose & mouth.
His tethered goat kneels
to eat scraps.

the cut stem
of the green papaya
drips milk

tiny spiders

spin
unnoticed

delicate webs
invisible

in rafters
and doorways

light touches
them

they seem
weightless

catching
dust

in time
they will darken

Solitary path, dust.
Cockcrow sounds far.
All is lost, gained.
Sunrise on the river.

A boy stands on the
parapet wall
in warm, light rain.

With a rusty billhook
he cuts the stem
of a green papaya,

and cradles
the large dripping
fruit.

Across the field,
a man shouts.
Crows fly, cawing.

nearing dusk
crystalline
birdsong

Rain cupped in a
fallen leaf.

Pebble, frond,
treepie.

On my way to the post office,
I see a dark-skinned man
cutting fodder in the hot sun.

Crows fly over the field.
Their shadows.

names of dragonflies

myristica sapphire
crimson marsh glider
dark daggerhead
forest spreadwing
goan shadowdancer

Squatting naked
in the warm dust,
a small boy plays
with his penis.

River-washed sheets
spread on
bushes
to dry in the sun.

Hazy sun.
Smoke from a leaf fire
drifts over the wall.
Pigeons strut on
roof tiles.

Silent lightning
in the east.
Dark sky.

A palm civet's claws
scrape
the metal roof.

Walking to the
post office, I pass
a woman
washing clothes
in the canal.

It's early evening,
the harsh light
softens. Crows peck
at something in
the road.

Children go by in
white school
uniforms,
holding hands.

Each day we see their photographs in the newspaper. Laid-off migrant workers, stranded because of lockdown. They walk thousands of kilometres, some with small children, desperate to get home.

Storm clouds gather in the west.
Cormorants fly north
past the river.

Slow dusk. Egrets arise
from paddy fields.

The sky is clear. I no longer
think of America.

Sitting on veranda steps,
I look up at the stars.

The day ends. A line
of white egrets crosses
the evening sky.
Standing waist-deep
in the river,
I see a faint outline
of the Western Ghats.
I left long ago.
The years have passed
& my hair is white.
Yet people in the village
remember me.

The musicians
& singers
sit barefoot
on the floor.

There's a silence
in the music
that feels like
prayer.

Draw a
bucket

sprinkle
water

to lay
the dust.

Before bed, I step out
into the cool air
on the veranda.

Black sky. Stillness.
Smell of ozone.

The leathery wings
of a fruit bat
rustle in a tree.

Clouds hide the
lunar eclipse.

Night,
the cricket's
rasp,
rain.

the
root

of
the

word
is

the
breath

morning sky
the spare calligraphy
of crows

IV

a hundred years
half spent asleep
work, illness, worry
take up the rest

.

go around naked
beg from strangers
like a crow

you'll never be rid
of self-pride

.

old, bent,
toothless, half
deaf, nearly
blind
no one listens
anymore

no one cares

—after Bhartṛihari

12 AM

Candle
on the table.

A gecko
clings
to the wall.

the moon's light
each leaf a page
of the notebook

the dark
spreads

encloses

this

small
hard

red
seed

shines
like

lacquer

blue
flowers

on the narrow
path

drape
a rock wall

days
pass

we
forget

rain puddles
on the path
crow
flies below

someone
nearby
beating clothes
stops

10 PM

Heavy rain
splashes into the
kitchen.

Two candles lit
a third has gone out.
Hours of rain.

Bat shelters on a
dark rafter out on
the veranda.

sun
rain

coco-
nut

crashes
on

tin
roof

I asked my neighbour to translate what
his small daughter said pointing
at the flood waters:

'It's the colour of milk tea.'

Immaculate
as the lotus,
this waterlily
rises from
the mud.

In a field behind
the roadside
fish market,
an abandoned bus
taken by vines.

the singing
of birds
is part of
the silence

rain all afternoon
paths become streams

the heart
can hear

the window looks north as crows cross the sky

leaf
cup full
of
rain

red, green,
yellow, gray,
orange

lichen

mud path
paved
with leaves

that
singleness,

the
one,

unreflecting
light

rain hidden moon

re-
flected,

the in-
finite

flame

rain falling straight down in silvery light

a line of ants

long shadows
on dried
mud

ash, dust

moss & lichen

constellations
moving

in the trees

the path
skirts
a field

rucksack
hung
from a tree

The fish monger
rides past
on his Hercules
bicycle.

He rings his bell.

A tethered goat
pulls grass
by the gate.

I sit on the steps
swatting mosquitoes.

A drongo sweeps past
the veranda.

I sit in a cane chair
and watch morning light
fill the trees.

Lorries honk on the
nearby road. A baby cries
next door.

Hair white,
old, alone on the
east-facing
veranda.

I see the Dipper
tilt just above
the trees.

we meet
again

after twenty
years

his old
smile

missing
teeth

sweeping ants,
sand,

cobwebs

iridescent
blue-

black
feathers

Drongos perch
on electric
wires strung
like cobwebs in
the trees. Under
a gray sky
I drift
toward sleep.

pond heron
flies away
once
it's seen

(among the wonders)

death after
death the
whole world
dies

yet no one
knows
how to die

—after Kabir

the wind
dies
at dusk

moon

nimbus
of

pearl

Talentless,
old, gratefully
I shed
expectations.

The day wanes.

My neighbour is singing
off-key.

fruit
bats

fly
west

brief
rain

settles
the

dust

Stayed away
all these
years.

Now return
is like a dream.

Sultry night. Flying
ants swarm.
The lamp on my desk
and a light in the neighbour's window
are the only lights
in the world.

AUTHOR'S NOTES

I was drawn to India as a boy after discovering my namesake in Kipling's famous novel. I first visited Kerala in 1976. Subsequently, I travelled there several times until the early 2000s. After many years, I returned in 2019. These notes are inspired by classical Japanese literature, especially the poetic travel diaries of Bashō.

*

The epigraph is from *The First Philosophers of Greece*, translated by Arthur Fairbanks, 1898.

The line quoted on page 45 is from the poem 'Nocturnal' by Lewis Thompson (1909–1949).

The poems that appear in Section I of this collection were first published in *Reliquiae*, Vol 8 No 1. Some of the poems in Section IV originally appeared in a chapbook, *the color of milk tea*, published by Otata's Bookshelf in 2019. Other poems appeared in issues of the journal *Otata*. I am grateful to the editor, John Martone.

www.ingramcontent.com/pod-product-compliance
Lightning Source LLC
Chambersburg PA
CBHW071625080526
44588CB00010B/1270